Keeping your chil on iPad and iPhone

© 2023 iTandCoffee

iOS/iPadOS 16 Edition

Special Sales and Supply Queries

For any information about buying this title in bulk quantities, or for supply of this title for educational or fund-raising purposes, contact iTandCoffee on **1300 885 420** or email **enquiry@itandcoffee.com.au**.

iTandCoffee classes and private appointments

For queries about classes and private appointments with iTandCoffee, call **1300 885 420** or email **enquiry@itandcoffee.com.au**.

iTandCoffee operates in and around Camberwell, Victoria in Australia.

Introducing iTandCoffee ...

iTandCoffee is a Melbourne-based business that was founded in 2012, by IT professional Lynette Coulston.

Lynette and the staff at iTandCoffee have a passion for helping others - especially women of all ages - to enter and navigate the new, and often daunting, world of technology and to utilise technology to make life easier, not harder!

At iTandCoffee, **patience is our virtue.**

You'll find a welcoming smile, a relaxed cup of tea or coffee, and a genuine enthusiasm for helping you to gain the confidence to use and enjoy your technology.

With personalised appointments and small, friendly classes – either remotely, in our bright, comfortable, cafe-style space or at your own place - we offer a brand of technology support and education that is so hard to find.

At iTandCoffee, you won't find young 'techies' who speak in a foreign language and move at a pace that leaves you floundering and 'bamboozled'!

Our focus is on helping you to use your technology in a way that enhances your personal and/or professional life – to feel more informed, organised, connected, and entertained!

Call on iTandCoffee for help with all sorts of technology – Apple, Windows, Android, iCloud, Evernote, OneDrive, Office 365, Dropbox, all sorts of other Apps, getting you set up on the internet, setting up a printer, and so much more.

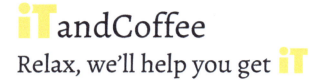

iTandCoffee
Relax, we'll help you get iT

If you are in small business, iTandCoffee has can help in so many ways – with amazing affordable solutions for your business information needs and marketing.

Here are just some of the topics covered in our regular classes:

- Microsoft Office Products and Microsoft 365 – OneDrive, Word, Excel, PowerPoint
- Introduction to the iPad and iPhone
- A Guided Tour of the Apple Watch
- Bring your Busy Life under Control using your technology.
- Getting to know your Mac and The Photos app on the Mac
- Understanding and using iCloud
- An Organised Life with Evernote
- Taking and Managing photos on the iPhone and iPad
- Managing Photos on a Windows computer
- Windows basics
- Travel with your iPad, iPhone, and other technology.
- Staying Safe Online
- Making the most of your personal technology in your business

The iTandCoffee website (itandcoffee.com.au) offers a wide variety of resources for those brave enough to venture online to learn more: handy hints for iPad, iPhone, and Mac; videos and slideshows of iTandCoffee classes; guides on a range of topics; a blog covering all sorts of topical events.

We also produce a regular Handy Hint newsletter full of information that is of interest to our clients and subscribers.

Hopefully, that gives you a bit of a picture of iTandCoffee and what we are about. Please don't hesitate to contact iTandCoffee to discuss our services or to make a booking.

We hope you enjoy this guide and find its contents informative and useful. Please feel free to offer feedback at feedback@itandcoffee.com.au.

Regards,

Lynette Coulston (iTandCoffee Founder)

Keeping your children safe on iPad and iPhone

TABLE OF CONTENTS

TABLE OF CONTENTS (cont.)

TABLE OF CONTENTS (cont.)

Introduction

About this guide

This guide has been written based on the '**Keeping Kids Safe on iPads and iPhones** information session that is regularly run by iTandCoffee.

This class and guide have been developed to assist parents in managing their child's use of their Apple mobile device/s, in terms of setting up parental controls and the 'Screen Time' settings, managing passwords, and some of the features and apps that parents should understand before giving their child a device that is actually a very powerful computer.

The guide is not intended to cover the broader topic of 'Cybersafety', as this tends to be covered on a regular basis by schools, in sessions run for parents.

This guide is specifically about how to put in place controls on Apple mobile devices.

We do not seek to cover setting up parental controls on any other type of device or computer or using any third-party apps and services.

iTandCoffee has many other guides on all sorts of other technology topics. Visit **itandcoffee.com.au/guides** to see this range.

In your own household ...

Do you struggle to manage your child's use of their technology? Do the kids know more about their (any maybe your) tech than you? Does your little hacker know your passcode?

Are there regular arguments over screen time? Are they impacting your relationship with your child?

Has your child snuck a device into their room overnight?

Has your child accessed inappropriate content? Is your child on social media already?

If you answered yes to any of the above questions, then rest assured - you have a very normal household in this age of personal technology!

Introduction

Shut the gate before that horse bolts!

While this is guide is certainly not intended as a parenting guide, as a mother of 4 and an IT educator, I do have a firm belief that when it comes to technology, it is essential that rules, expectations, limitations, and boundaries are established and upheld from a very early age – as soon as the child starts using technology.

With my own children, their technology was always a privilege – not a right. And their access to that technology was conditional on them adhering to rules about its use. Breaches of these rules resulted in temporary loss of devices or access to certain apps/services.

Remember that even those hand-me-down iPhones and iPads need to be locked down to ensure that your naturally inquisitive child cannot access content and features that are inappropriate to their age.

And don't forget about your own devices, Grandma's device, Uncle John's device and the devices belonging to your child's friends.

Any device that they use should have in place parental controls that are appropriate for your child's age.

It only takes one device with inadequate controls to give your child access to content that, once seen, can never be unseen; content that may open doors than can never again be closed.

Let's talk first about passwords ...

Should your child have your iTunes & App Store/iCloud password?

In many households, it is often relatively young children who know the passwords to parents' devices and accounts.

In many cases, the children can remember the passwords that Mum and Dad can't, and parents often rely on a child as the keeper of the household password/s.

But should your children know these passwords?

I would suggest not, especially in the case of your Apple account, and especially if your credit card is linked to that account.

Would you give your credit card to your child and let him/her loose in a toy store? Probably not!

If a child has your Apple password, there is the potential to spend an incredibly large amount of money in very little time. It happens on a very regular basis!

There are apps valued at around $1000 (or more) in the App store, and this doesn't even in include 'in app purchases' which can be huge in value.

In-App Purchases (which we will discuss later) can quickly add up – some are hundreds of dollars.

If you are the keeper of the keys (i.e. only you know the password), you can vet what your children are downloading and purchasing, and control where money is spent.

Even better, set them up with their own *'child'* Apple ID – instead of using your own Apple ID for **Media and Purchases** on their device/s – and make them part of your *iCloud Family*.

You will then be able to manage their 'screen time' and app downloads/purchases more effectively – and even remotely, from your own device.

We will look at this whole area of families and Apple IDs in a later section of this document.

Let's talk first about passwords ...

A secret password might not be enough!

Did you know that, after you put in your password for the **Media and Purchases**, your child might have the next 15 minutes to go on a spending spree? Without a password!

There are so many 'Free' games that entice users to 'buy' digital things that are not actually free.

Sometimes, it is not obvious that there is a cost involved.

This has caught out many parents who, thinking that the game their child is playing was free, just keep re-entering their password for their child so that they can, say, purchase accessories for their virtual pet store!

I have met numerous people whose children have spent well over $1000 in one or two days. For one family, the spend was around $6000.

We will shortly look at how this can be easily prevented.

What about all those other passwords and passcodes?

While we are on the topic of passwords, I would recommend that your children should never have access to any of your passwords/passcodes for accounts and devices – your passcode to your own phone, your computer password, your mail password, and a variety of other passwords.

If they know your iPad or iPhone passcode, they may also be able to view all your other account passwords. If your own device doesn't have parental controls, the door could be open to your child accessing content you have not allowed on their own device/s.

While your child remembering these passwords on your behalf and being able to access your device may seem innocent and safe while that child is young, my personal experience in dealing with families and technology over many years is this can all-too-often lead to issues as time goes by.

Our firm belief at iTandCoffee is that it is a good idea to establish boundaries on this when they are younger.

Set up separate 'user accounts' on the computer to 'rope off' the kids from your parental account. Then, for the children's account/s, you can establish parental controls - to ensure that they only access appropriate content and features.

Let's talk first about passwords ...

But where can you store all those passwords?

We can all end up with a very long list of passwords, for all sorts of accounts and devices.

Many people choose to write down their passwords in a book or on a piece of paper, and (perhaps) store this document/book in a place where they hope the kids won't find it.

Others store passwords in Notes or in Contacts on their i-Device, or perhaps in a file on the computer.

A safer approach is to use a 'password keeper' app like **1Password, Lastpass,** or **Dashlane** on your iPad or iPhone (and on your computer). Each of these apps now operate under a subscription model and provide access to your passwords from all your devices.

An app such as this allows you to store all passwords, and gain access to these passwords using a single 'master password'. That way, all you ever need to remember is that master password.

This makes your passwords a lot more secure than using any of the other options listed earlier, and less prone to discovery by prying little eyes.

You can even consider using the standard Notes app on the iPad/iPhone/Mac, which includes a 'Lock' feature for Notes that contain sensitive information.

For any of these solutions, it is essential that you remember the master password that you set – as you may lose access to your stored passwords if that master password is not known.

Do you know your child's password/s?

It is a good idea for parents to insist that they know your child's password/s and passcode/s, especially when they are young.

Pop them in your own Password Safe with all your other passwords. And we will look soon at how you can now ensure (via Screen Time) that your child can't change their own device Passcode without your permission.

Especially when young, our belief is that children should know that you can and will check their emails, texts, photos, and Safari web browsing history at any time.

This (of course) becomes more of a privacy issue when the kids reach the teen years, but it is worth considering setting that expectation of 'spot checks' for as long as you can get away with it!

Introducing Parental Controls on Apple Mobile Devices

Introducing Screen Time

On Apple mobile devices running iOS 12 and later, Parental Controls are set up in an area of the **Settings** app called **Screen Time**.

This replaced the previous **Restrictions** area that applied in earlier versions of iOS (which was found in the General option of Settings).

Screen Time allows a parent to

- Establish a day-by-day **Downtime** schedule for when some or all apps are blocked on the device
- Set **App Limits** on how much time the child can spend on different categories of apps (e.g. Social, Games, Entertainment …), on sets of apps or on individual apps.
- Set up **Communication Limits** to limit who your child can communicate with and when – you can control their Contacts!
- Nominate certain apps as **Always Allowed** so that they are not impacted by **Downtime** and **App Limits.**
- See **Weekly Reports** on the child's device usage – time used, number of notifications, number of pickups, for both apps and websites.
- Establish **Content and Privacy Restrictions** such as limiting content by age rating, disabling key features and apps, restricting adult websites, ensuring privacy protection, and locking down other important settings (as previously provided in the **Restrictions** settings of earlier versions of iOS).

All Power to the Parent - Remote Management!

A great feature also introduced in iOS 12 in 2018 is the ability to manage a child's **Screen Time** across ALL their Apple mobile devices – all from the parent's device.

Introducing Parental Controls on Apple Mobile Devices

This is possible for families that have established an iCloud Family, where the children's devices are managed by the 'parent' of the family. We cover setting up such a 'family' later in this guide.

If you haven't set up such an iCloud Family, Screen Time controls can still be set up and managed on a device-by-device basis (ie. directly, on your child's device).

Protecting access to Screen Time Settings

When you set up **Screen Time** for your child from your own device, or on your child's device itself, you will be able to set a **Screen Time Passcode**.

Setting such a passcode is essential for ensuring that your child cannot undo/change the settings that you establish.

This passcode MUST be one that your children can never guess – and it will be one that they will almost certainly want to 'hack', so be very careful whenever you enter it to ensure they are not watching.

As an example, one parent I spoke to was tricked by her 11-year-old into entering that passcode in the kitchen, while standing in front of the oven. The child watched the passcode entry in the oven door reflection! Within a week, the child had downloaded an inappropriate app and was being targeted by a predator via that app's messaging service. An extreme case, I know – but a great example of what can happen when controls are not in place and how keen a child can be to bypass any controls.

It is highly recommended that you use a different passcode to your device's 'unlock' passcode as, if your child is like most children, they will most likely watch you enter this passcode regularly and inevitably work out what it is!

A big word of warning: Do not forget this Screen Time passcode!

If this passcode is forgotten, you may not be able to change the **Screen Time** settings or reset/wipe the device.

(Note. From iOS/iPad 14, Apple has added the capability to turn on a setting that allows you to reset your Screen Time Passcode using your Apple ID and Password. We will cover this a bit later.)

Turning on Screen Time

Finding screen Time

Screen Time can be found in **Settings** on any iPhone or iPad (running iOS 12 or later.

Some aspects of Screen Time can only be set up on the child's device. But a large number of the Screen Time settings can be controlled from the Parent device if an iCloud Family is in place – and can apply to <u>all</u> devices belonging to the child.

When you activate **Screen Time**, you are stepped through the different options to get started

You can then come back later and refine your selections – for example, to set different **App Limits** by category of app or by individual app.

Setting up Screen Time on the child's device

If you are setting up Screen Time on your child's device, tap the **Turn on Screen** Time option to get started.

Turning on Screen Time

Choose **Continue,** then **This Is My Child's iPhone** (iPad)

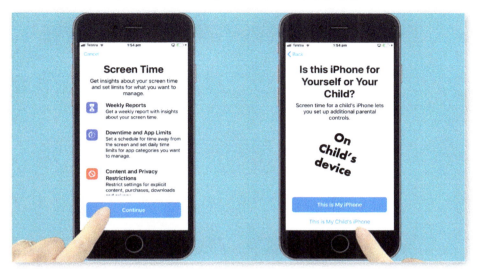

Set up Screen Time from your own (Parent) device

If you are setting up your child's Screen Time from your own (parent) device, your child must already be part of your iCloud family – in which case you will see their name listed in the **Screen Time** settings, in a section titled **Family**.

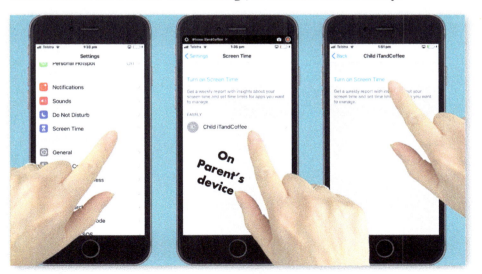

Tap on their name, then tap **Turn on Screen Time** (see image on next page).

New Setup Steps in iOS/iPadOS 16

In iOS/iPadOS 16, Apple has provided a couple of new helpful steps at the start of the setup 'wizard'.

It should be noted that, with each step of the setup 'wizard', the **Set Up Later** can be chosen to defer any setup until later.

The first screen that now appears when you choose **Turn on Screen Time** is one that allows you to enable a default suggested set of Content Restrictions that are based on the age of the child. These restrictions relate to apps, entertainment content, web content, and more.

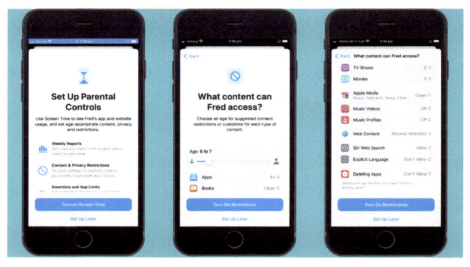

Tap on any of the options shown and customise the defaults that have been provided.

If you increase the age that is shown, the Content Restriction settings will adjust accordingly.

When you are happy with the settings that have been applied here, choose **Turn on Restrictions**.

New – Protect Sensitive Photos

The next step of the setup 'wizard' provides a new parental control that is designed to protect children against sharing inappropriate image via the Messages app.

It is important to note that this control does not prevent the child from sharing sensitive photos via a third party app. But is is certainly worth turning on as part of the setup, or later from the Screen Time settings

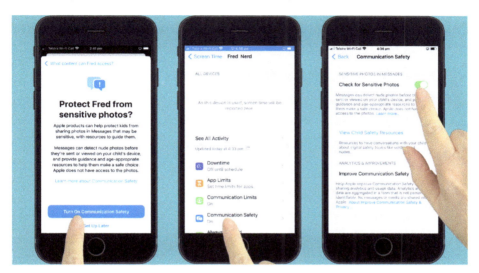

Next, Set up Downtime

The next of the setup steps is **Downtime** – to set a daily schedule for deactivating apps on your child's device.

Typically, this will be from before bedtime until the morning.

As part of the initial setup, Downtime will be set to apply to every day. We'll look shortly at how this can then be customised by day of week.

Simply choose the **Start** time, then the **End** time and choose **Turn On Downtime** to to complete this step.

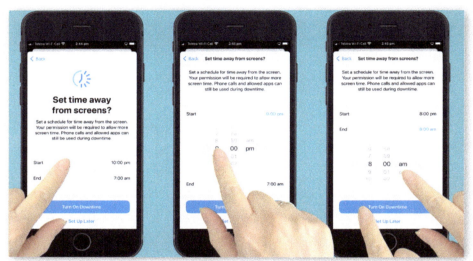

The image on the right shows an example of what the Home Screen looks like with Downtime active.

Only apps that are specifically nominated as **Always Allowed** (which we will cover soon) are available.

All other apps are greyed and unable to be opened.

If you would rather leave this step for now and come back to it later, choose the **Not Now** option at the bottom.

Then Set App Limits

The next step is to set time limits for all apps or for categories of apps.

At the time of writing this guide, the available app categories are Social Networking, Games, Entertainment, Education, Creativity, Productivity and Finance, Information & Reading, Health & Fitness, Utilities, Shopping & Food, Travel and Other. There is also a Websites option to set limits for specific websites that you nominate.

I recommend to clients that you choose **Not Now** (at the bottom) for this step and come back to it later.

The single App Limit you are able to set at this point can only be by Category – or for all apps/categories.

When you set the App Limits later, you can set limits by individual apps or for a nominated set of apps, or for websites. We'll look at these options shortly.

If you do want to set the App Limits by category or for **All Apps and Categories,** tap the applicable option to tick it and then choose **Set**.

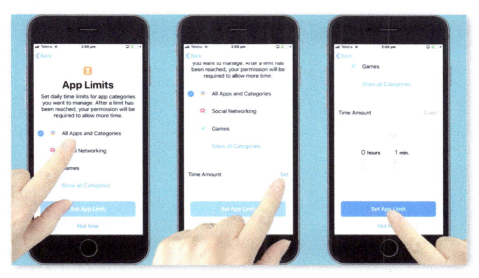

You can then choose the time limit that applies (using the hour and minute 'winders' that you see).

Once you have set the required time limit, tap **Set App Limit** to apply that limit – or choose **Not Now** to come back to this later.

Create a Screen Time Passcode

The next step in the Screen Time setup is to set up the Passcode for Screen Time for this child.

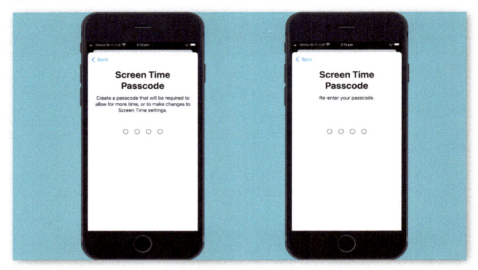

Enter, then re-enter the passcode to confirm.

What passcode should you use

As mentioned earlier, this Passcode MUST be one that kids don't know and that they can't guess. As also suggested earlier, it is recommended that this Passcode is different to your own device 's passcode.

If you have more than one child, this Passcode could be different for each child. But I suggest that you use the same Screen Time passcode for all children.

You will be required to enter the 4-digit passcode twice.

Passcode Recovery

If you are doing the Screen Time setup on the child's device, you will then be provided with the option to set up **Screen Time Passcode Recovery** using your own Apple ID.

Create a Screen Time Passcode

It is strongly recommended that you enable this feature, to avoid the possibility of being locked out of Screen Time settings due to a forgotten passcode.

(Note. This is one of the reasons why it is essential that your child does not know your Apple account password. If they do, they could change the Screen Time passcode that you set.)

If you don't wish to use the recovery feature, select **Cancel** at top left.

This will still allow you to establish the device's Screen Time Passcode but will warn you that you won't be able to re-set that passcode if you forget it.

Make sure you protect the device's Screen Time Passcode and, if you haven't enabled the Recovery option, **DON'T FORGET IT**!

Make sure you set up the Screen Time Passcode before your child does!

While you will be able to easily re-set the Screen Time Passcode for the children from your own device without being asked for the previous passcode, any change to the device's Screen Time Passcode when on that device requires authentication of the previous Passcode (or use of the Recovery option if that was enabled at the time of setting the device's Screen Time Passcode).

If your child beats you to setting up the device's Screen Time Passcode – and then forgets the passcode or is unwilling to provide the passcode to you – you will be locked out of that device's Screen Time settings for good.

And once again, the fact that your child can change or turn off the Screen Time passcode from your own device (assuming you have an iCloud Family setup) is another good reason why you child should never be granted unsupervised access to your parental device.

What if the Screen Time Passcode is forgotten?

If the device's Screen Time Passcode is forgotten or unknown AND the recovery option is not in place (which will be the case for device Screen Time Passcodes set up prior to iOS/iPadOS 14) then the only way to re-gain access to the Screen Time settings for the device is to wipe the device and set it up afresh.

If resetting the device is just not an option – perhaps because of valuable data that would be lost - there are also computer-based Apps that can be purchased to 'hack' this Passcode. This is usually achieved by taking a backup of the device to the computer, then accessing an option in the purchased app that uses 'brute force' to work out the Screen Time Passcode. (Don't tell the kids this one!)

Now you are ready to customise Screen Time

Setting the Screen Time Passcode ends the 'setup wizard' steps.

You will be left on a screen that shows the full set of Screen Time options that you will see each time you look at the child's Screen Time.

You can now go through each of these options in turn to further customize the Screen Time controls.

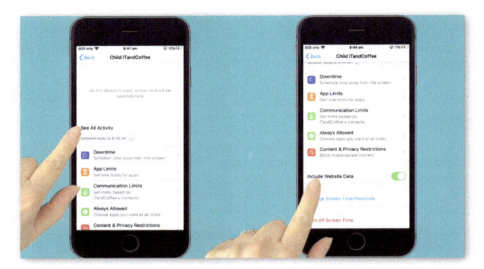

The top section of the screen will show a graphic representing your child's device usage.

This will be blank initially. From this point forward, data will be collected about the child's usage of the device/s and this graphic will then be updated.

The other Screen Time options are listed below that.

At this point, it is best to ensure that the **Include Website Data** setting (if visible) is turned on – so that you can monitor time spent on Apps AND on websites.

You may also see the **Share Across Devices** option.

If you see this option, make sure that this is turned on, so that the combined Screen Time can be tracked across all devices.

Customise Downtime by Day

Let's look further at **Downtime** now.

When you initially set the Downtime **From** and **To** time, the Downtime will set to apply to **Every Day**.

Once you have done this initial setup, you will then have option to customise Downtime by day of week – i.e. the **Customise Days** option will then become available.

Tap this **Customise Days** option to see the schedule for each day of the week, which is initially set to the Downtime schedule you had set up for **Every Day**.

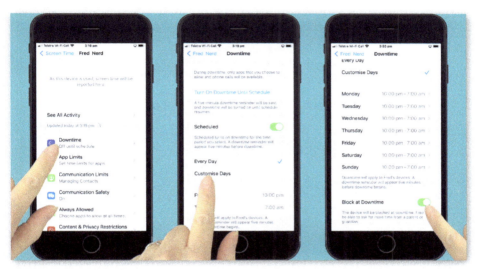

Simply tap each day and choose the **Start** and **End** time for **Downtime** on that day of the week.

Each day then, your child will get a reminder 5 minutes before **Downtime** starts.

Make sure that the **Block at Downtime** switch is turned to On (green on left) to ensure that the child no longer access un-authorised apps and content.

Hopefully that will reduce those regular arguments about technology in the leadup to bedtime!

Set App Limits

As mentioned earlier, App Limits can be set for

- All Apps/categories
- A whole category of apps (e.g. Social, Games, ...)
- A set of apps that you nominate
- Individual apps
- A specific website

To start, tap the **App Limits** option in Screen Time, then tap **Add Limit.**

To apply a limit to a whole category of apps, tap the circle on the left of that category.

Alternatively, expand the category by tapping the > on the right.

This will provide a list of all the Apps that are within that category and allow for one or more specific apps to be selected.

Once the categories and/or apps you wish to limit have been selected, choose **Next** at top right.

Set the time limit using the 'winders' that appears.

Set App Limits

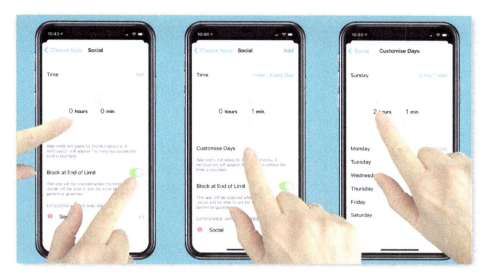

You will see the option to **Block at End of Limit** beneath the time area.

Make sure you turn this on if you see it - assuming you want to have the app/s (or website) automatically blocked when the limit is reached.

As soon as you have set a time greater than zero for the limit, you will see the **Customise Days** option appear below the 'winder' area. This will then allow you to set different 'day of week' App Limits for that app or set of apps.

Once you have set up each day's App Limit (or a single limit applicable to all days), tap **Add** at top right. Then then **Add Limit** to set up Limits.

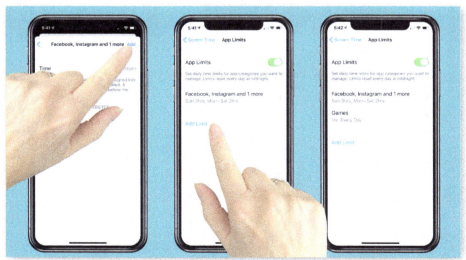

Set App Limits

To later change an App Limit, choose the **App Limits** option from Screen Time, then tap the applicable item in the list of 'limits' that have been set.

You can then adjust the apps that are included in the limit, change the times and **Customise Days**.

You can even temporarily turn off an individual App Limit or all App Limits if required.

We'll shortly look at another way that you can set App Limits – where you can see which apps/websites are being 'over-used' by your child and apply limits to those specific apps.

'Always Allowed' Apps

If there are apps that need to be available all the time – that should not be impacted by Downtime or App Limits - add them to the **Always Allowed** list.

Tap **Always Allowed** in Screen Time. The top section of the **Always Allowed** area shows those apps that are the **Allowed Apps** (i.e. exempt from limits).

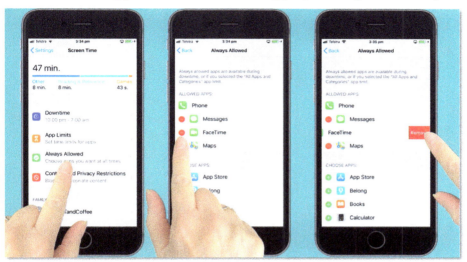

Tap ⊖ to remove an app from the **Allowed Apps** set (or swipe from right to left).

Use ⊕ to add a new **Allowed Apps** app from the CHOOSE APPS section – i.e. to move it from the bottom section up to the top.

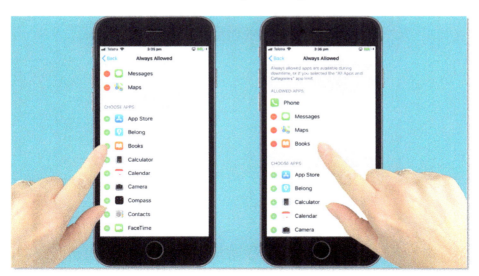

Monitor their Screen Time

Once Screen Time is set up, your child's device usage will be tracked and reported in the top section of the Screen Time settings area.

The graphic at the top will give a summary of the child's daily device usage, and you can find out more about this usage by selecting **See All Activity**.

This will give the option to view usage by Week, or by Day.

Below the graphic is a section that shows **Most Used** apps, which can be viewed by category or by app/website.

Monitor their Screen Time

When viewing the 'Most Used' apps/websites/categories, you can then tap on a particular item in the list (for example, one that shows excessive usage) and choose the **Add Limit** from there.

Beneath the **Most Used** section are other sections that show the details of **Pickups** (and the app that was first accessed after pickup) and **Notifications** by app.

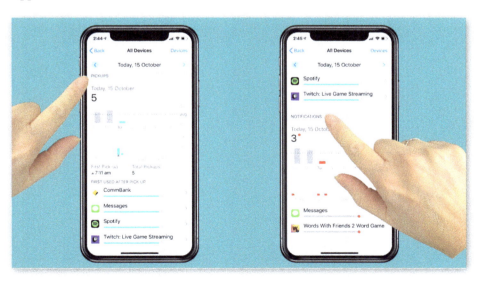

Monitor their Screen Time

For the apps listed in the Notifications section, you can then (for some) choose to change the settings relating to the App's notifications – so that your child receives less distracting and unnecessary notifications from apps.

You can turn off sounds, disable banners and more.

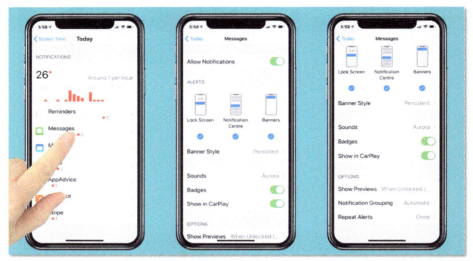

Now you can control their Contacts

Early in 2020, some new controls were added to Screen Time – called **Communication Limits**.

Communication Limits allow you to control who your child can communicate with during the day, and during Downtime

This will impact who can contact your child (or be contacted by your child) for Messages, Phone, Mail and Facetime.

This area of Screen Time also allows you to monitor and manage your child's Contacts list.

You will see there is the **During Allowed Screen Time** option, for nominating allowed Contacts during the day.

This can be set to Everyone (i.e. allowing calls, texts, emails etc. from people not in Contacts) or **Contacts Only** (to protect your child from contact with unknown people).

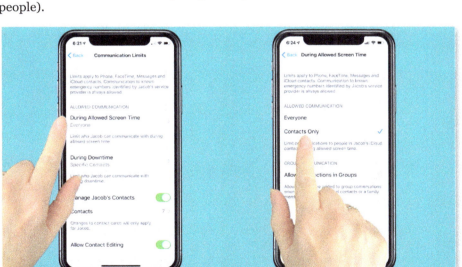

In the **During Downtime** option of **Communication Limits**, you can set even tighter controls over who can be in contact with your child overnight, when Downtime is active.

During Downtime, the list of people who can make contact with your child (or be contacted by your child) can be set to **Contacts Only** (which is the default when Downtime is active) or to **Specific Contacts** – which would typically be just Mum and Dad, and perhaps other family members.

Now you can control their Contacts

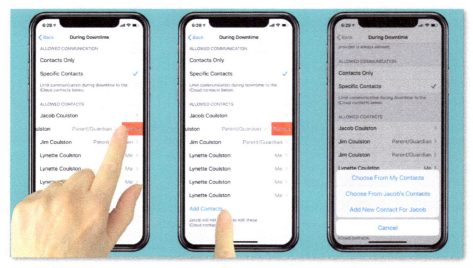

If **Specific Contacts** is chosen, the bottom section then allows the selection of which Contacts should be included in this list. New Contacts can be added to this list, either from the child's Contacts list or (if the setup is being done from the parent's device) from the parent's own list of Contacts.

Communication Limits also includes the capability to take over management of the child's Contacts list – by turning on **Manage *child-name's* Contacts**.

Tap **Contacts** under that to manage the list of contacts. And decide whether or not the child is allowed to edit the Contacts list – by turning on (or not) the **Allow Contact Editing** option.

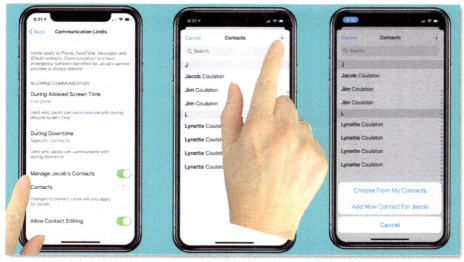

Content & Privacy Restrictions

The next area is a biggie – and contains essential parental controls that should be established for **every** child.

It is called **Content and Privacy Restrictions** and replaces the **Restrictions** area that used to apply prior to iOS 12 (which was previously found in **Settings -> General**).

When you tap on **Content and Privacy Restrictions** for the first time, you will notice that all the options are 'greyed'.

You must first turn on **Content & Privacy Restrictions** to enable the various options.

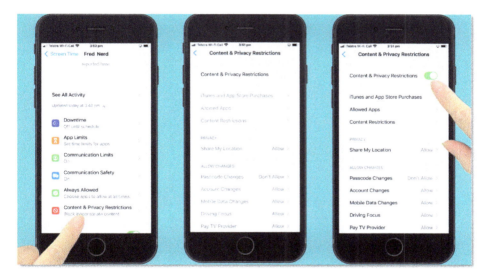

Then it is a matter of going through each option and making decisions about what to limit and what to allow.

iTunes and App Store Purchases

In this option, you can control whether the following is allowed:

• Installing Apps   • Deleting Apps   • In-app Purchases

and what restriction applies for purchases of Apps, Books, iTunes – whether the iTunes/Apple ID password is required every time or not. The options for each are:

• Always Required   • Don't Require

In this area, I would recommend that you tap on **In App Purchases** and choose **Don't Allow** and that the **Require Password** option is set to **Always Required.**

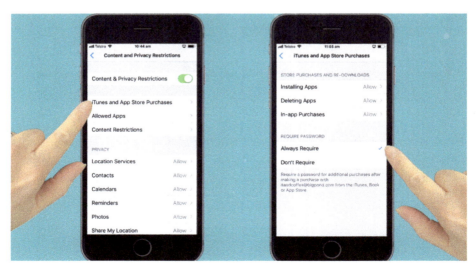

What Standard Apps are Allowed?

This next option in **Content and Privacy Restrictions** is the **Allowed Apps** option.

The options shown in **Allowed Apps** cater for limiting the standard Apps and features that can/can't be used on the restricted device.

For example, you can choose to optionally turn off Safari (for web browsing), Camera, Facetime, Siri, Airdrop, and other apps/services.

To turn off a particular feature (to prevent its use), just slight the circle from the right side to the left. Green means 'on', not green means 'off'.

Any apps that you disable here will still remain on the device/s – they won't be deleted.

They will simply be hidden from the Home Screen and their functions will not be accessible.

For example, if Mail is turned off here, the Share menu will no longer show Mail as a Share option.

Content Restrictions

Allowed Store Content

The **Content Restrictions** section of **Content and Privacy Restrictions** allows for a limiting of the 'rating' of content that can be viewed, is downloaded to, and accessed on, the device.

First, set up the Country applicable to Age Classifications.

Then tap on each option to set up the 'Ratings' applicable to your child and your child's age. For **Music, Podcasts and News** and **Books**, choose **Clean** to block explicit language.

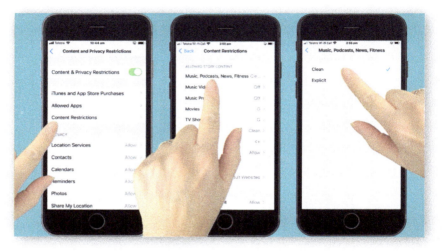

For **Movies** and **TV Shows**, choose the applicable maximum age level – so if you want them to only be able to watch anything up to and including M, tap M.

Content Restrictions

In the **Apps** option, choose the maximum age level allowed. This will then stop apps for higher age levels from even being visible in the App Store. Apps that exceed the limit chosen will not even be visible in the App Store.

Apps can even be disallowed completely – by choosing **Don't Allow Apps**.

This can offer a quick and easy way of enforcing a 'time out', where only the standard apps are visible on the Home Screen and all other downloaded apps magically disappear! The apps are still present on the device but are just hidden (as shown in rightmost image above).

Content Restrictions

Web Content

This one is a 'must do'!

The Web Content option in Content Restrictions allows you to limit the type of websites that your child can access using Safari. It also limits what images they see in searches – which is so important.

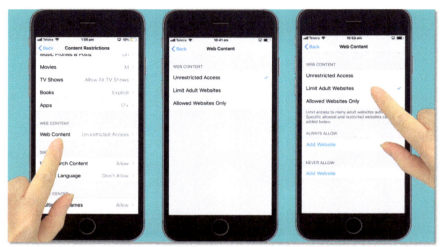

As a very minimum, make sure you select **Limit Adult Websites** in this section. By choosing **Limit Adult Websites**, the device will not be able to access any website that is deemed by Apple to be potentially unsafe for children.

Alternatively – and especially for younger children - the stricter option of **Allowed Websites Only** allows you to build up a very limited list of 'safe websites'.

Content Restrictions

For both the **Limit Adult Websites** and the **Allowed Websites Only** options, forced tracking of Safari history is enabled automatically.

In Safari, there will no longer be the option to clear browsing history – the **Clear** option (found in the Bookmarks option, in the 'history' section) will be greyed

This restriction will also prevent your child from using the **Private** browsing feature of Safari – a browsing mode that prevents any history from being tracked.

The **Private** option will no longer appear when you choose the 'double-box' symbol (that allows you to manage your Safari tabs). The right-most image below shows the list of options that appear when you view the **Tab Groups** option from Safari – showing it excludes the Private option if you restrict Web Content.

Content Restrictions

Whenever the iPad or iPhone is asked to access a website that has not been deemed 'safe', a message will pop up advising that the website is restricted.

The child can simply ask the parent to tap the Allow Website option to enable that web page and add it to the list of '*allowed*' websites from that point on.

All that is required is the entry of the applicable **Screen Time Password**.

The website will then be added to a list of websites that are deemed to be 'safe' for the child, allowing the child access to the website from that point forward.

To block access to that website in future, go into **Screen Time -> Content Restrictions -> Web Content**, and remove that website from the list of allowed websites.

To remove a website from the 'Allowed' list, swipe left on the website that you wish to disallow and select the delete option that appears in red. This ensures that the child gets the '***restricted***' message if the website is accessed again in future.

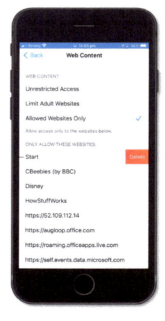

Content Restrictions

With the **Limit Adult Content** option in '***Always Allow***', just be aware that this **will not limit access to content on sites like YouTube** (if you have allowed the YouTube website).

This may mean that your child can still access very inappropriate content from YouTube.

To 'turn off' access to a website site such as this, add it to the **Never Allow** section by choosing 'Add a Website', and typing in the URL of the website you wish to block (for example, **www.youtube.com**).

A warning about third-party Web Browser apps

Make sure you don't allow any Web Browser app other than Safari on your child's device, as the parental controls that you set up in Screen Time will only impact Safari.

Kids will often want to download Chrome or Google (or some other web browser) as an alternative app to Safari – something that should not be necessary.

These Apps are not managed by Apple's Restrictions – so the door is open for them to access inappropriate content if parental controls are not separately set up for that web browser (something that we are not going to cover as part of this guide).

Siri

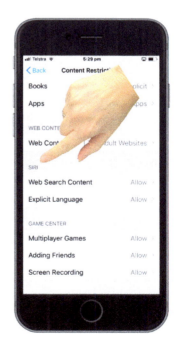

The **Siri** sub-section of **Content Restrictions** allows you to prevent Siri from allowing, speaking, or writing explicit language.

Tap the **Explicit Language** option and choose **Don't Allow** – and then **Siri** will instead use asterisks to cover up swear words and 'bleep' bad language.

By choosing **Don't Allow** in the **Web Search Content** option, you can block searching of the Web using Siri – especially if you have Safari blocked or restricted.

If you leave this set to **Allow**, your child may be able to search for content that you otherwise have prevented.

Content Restrictions

Game Centre

Game Centre allows the i-Device user to play multi-player games with friends, and to send and receive invitations for 'friends' to play these games together. It keeps 'leader boards' so that players can compare their scores.

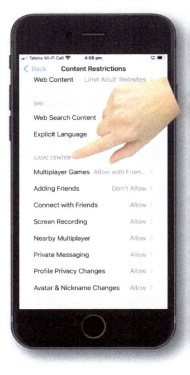

The **Game Centre** section of restrictions allows for the restricting of whether **Multiplayer Games** are enabled, and whether the i-Device user can add friends.

On a younger child's i-Device, I suggest setting the **Adding Friends** option to **Don't Allow**, so that you are able to 'vet' friends before they are added.

Just temporarily **Allow Adding Friends** whenever you want to approve of the addition of a friend, then change it back to **Don't Allow** to stop future unapproved additions.

Screen Recording is a relatively new feature of the iOS and iPadOS devices that allows the user to record whatever is happening on the screen, and then save this video recording to their Photos library.

Kids are often keen to record their exploits in a game – and can use the Screen Recording feature to do this.

Some remote support apps (for example Zoom, TeamViewer and other remote support services) use this **Screen Recording** feature to 'broadcast' the device screen to someone else via the internet.

So, it is important to consider whether you want this Screen Recording and broadcasting feature to be available on your child's device, especially for young children - choose **Don't Allow** for this option to disable it.

There are also several other new iOS/iPadOS 16 options to consider – **Nearby Multiplayer**, **Private Messaging**, **Profile Privacy Changes**, and **Avatar & Nickname Changes**.

Content Restrictions

For most of these, you will probably choose **Don't Allow** – at least initially. Then you can negotiate relaxing any of them when your child comes across a game that is not doing what they want!

A warning ...

Many games allowing for multiple players and for communication between players are not controlled by the **Content Restrictions** you have established in this **Game Centre** section.

So, make sure you understand what capabilities are included in any game (or other app) used by a child before allowing them to download, install and use that app.

Even apps like **Words with Friends** can be dangerous on a child's device – as there is the capability to play games with and communicate with total strangers.

Protecting your Child's Privacy

The **Privacy** section of **Content and Privacy Restrictions** deals with protecting the privacy of the device user.

It is important to note that the Privacy Restrictions **must be set up on each individual device belonging to the child**. They cannot be set up from the parent's device.

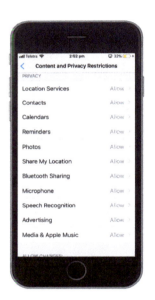

This section is where you can control what apps are able to use certain information and features of the device, and what privacy-related features should be enabled and disabled.

For each of the listed items in the **Privacy** section, you will have the option to 'turn off' certain apps/features/services – thereby stopping that app/feature/service from using whichever data, feature, or service you have selected.

When this setup has been completed, tap on the **Don't Allow Changes** option at the top to lock in the privacy settings and prevent the child from changing the settings you have put in place (as shown below right for the **Location Services** option, which we'll cover next).

Of course, the **Privacy** settings can be established first outside the **Content and Privacy Restrictions** area - in **Settings -> Privacy** - where you will most of the same privacy options as those found in **Content and Privacy Restrictions**.

Let's look at a few of the areas of the **Privacy** section of **Content and Privacy Restrictions**.

Protecting your Child's Privacy

Location Services

Location Services allows apps and websites (including Maps, Camera, Weather, and other apps) to determine and perhaps record a device's location.

The **Privacy** section in **Restrictions** allows you to control which apps are allowed to use this service and record location data.

Tap on **Location Services** in the **Privacy** section.

Part-way down the screen, you will see a list of apps and features that want to use the device's location.

Tap on each app in turn and you will see a set of 3 or 4 options – **Never**, **Ask Next Time or When I Share**, **While Using the App** and (for some apps only) **Always**.

Choose **Never** if you do not want location information used or stored by that app or feature.

For those apps that you want to allow Location Services access, I would generally choose **While Using App** or **Ask Next Time or when I Share** instead of **Always** – at the very least to avoid unnecessary battery drainage.

Protecting your Child's Privacy

Precise Location

A new option was added in iOS 14, designed to further protect our privacy.

The **Precise Location** allows you to choose to only provide an approximate location to an app, instead of providing a **Precise Location**. If you do decide to allow an app to use the device's location, it is well worth turning off this setting on your child's device.

Should Camera store the device location?

One of the key apps to consider when it comes to Location Services is the Camera app. Do you want photos taken by your child to include the location?

While this can be great when you are travelling, there is always the danger that a child could inadvertently send a photo to someone that has their location stored in the photo's metadata (where metadata is 'background' data stored about every photo – location, date, time, camera and more).

At the very least, turn off **Precise Location** for this one – or to be really safe, change it to **Never**.

Should you switch off Location Services completely?

While it is tempting to turn **Location Services** OFF completely, you should consider leaving it on for a few of very important reasons.

If you want to enable the use of apps like Maps, Google Maps, public transport apps, and weather apps that can show the weather at your current location, you will need to leave Location Services on.

Location Services allows for the tracking of a lost or stolen device, and the 'remote wiping' of a device that cannot be found. It also allows a parent to track the location of a child.

These capabilities are delivered through the **Find My** app (new from iOS 13). The child must be signed in to iCloud for the **Find My iPhone/iPad** service to be available for that child's device/s– we will discuss this later in this guide.

Protecting your Child's Privacy

On the other hand, if you only want the device's location to be trackable in the case of loss – i.e. you don't want <u>any</u> tracking at any other time by <u>any</u> apps, it is OK to turn off Location Services.

When a device is put into Lost Mode (when it goes missing), Location Services will still turn on for the purpose of tracking the device when it is next connected to the internet.

Share my Location

Before we leave this discussion about Location Services and its Privacy settings, take a moment to consider if you would like your child to be able to share their current location via the **Messages** app, or perhaps another app called **Find My**

These apps make it very easy for a child to share their current location – even making it possible for this location to be dynamically updated as they move.

While this may be a useful feature for older children and adults, there is always the danger that your child could give away their exact location to someone they shouldn't. (Although the new Communication Limits can now provide you with control over who they can contact, perhaps rendering this less of a concern.)

The **Location Services** option in the **Privacy** section (both in the main area of **Settings** and in the **Content and Privacy Restrictions** area of Screen Time) provides the option to control whether the device location can be shared.

If you don't want your child sharing their location, tap on **Share My Location** option in the **Location Services** option of the **Privacy** section and turn off this setting using the switch at the top of that screen

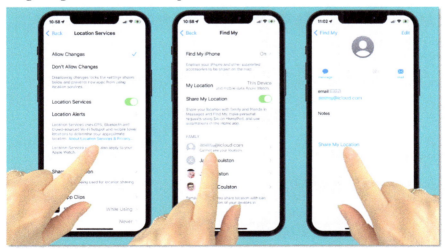

Protecting your Child's Privacy

You will still be able to share the child's location with iCloud Family members if that **Share my Location** switch is off.

The second section here allows for the nomination of which iCloud Family members can see the device's location, and which of the child's devices is used to provide this location to family members.

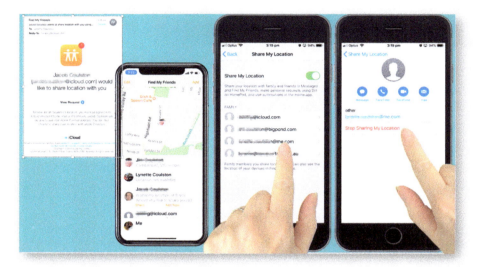

You will also notice that there is a **Share my Location** option in the main **Privacy** area of **Content and Privacy Restrictions** (as well as in the **Location Services** area).

The reason why it is separately listed is that you may want to **Not Allow** the **Share my Location** feature, but not restrict the other Location Services settings.

Lock in the Privacy Restrictions for Location

Once you have established the Location Services Privacy restrictions that will apply for the child's device, you must then 'lock them in' to prevent any changes by the child.

If you don't do this, the child can make their own changes to these settings from **Settings->Privacy**.

By choosing **Don't Allow Changes** at the top of the each privacy option in Screen Time (see next page for an example), the corresponding settings in **Settings -> Privacy** will be greyed/disabled – preventing unauthorized changes by your child.

Protecting your Child's Privacy

The same principle then applies for the other options in the Privacy section of **Content and Privacy Restrictions**: turn on or off certain apps/features, then lock in the settings with **Don't Allow Changes** at the top.

Where has your child been?

It may be useful to know that the **Settings -> Privacy** area on your child's device also includes a setting that is a bit buried. It is worth knowing of this area if you ever need to work out where your child has been.

Protecting your Child's Privacy

The device can track and record 'significant locations' – locations that your child visits and spends time at.

On child's device go to **Settings -> Privacy -> Location Services** and tap the **System Services** option that is at the bottom.

Scroll down and tap the **Significant Locations** option (see next page).

This will show a list of locations that your child has visited, the dates and times on which the place was visited, and for how long.

See next page for images that show the steps to finding this information.

(Please note that, at the time of writing this guide, the Significant Locations feature has a bug and is not currently showing any detail of the recent locations. Hopefully this issue will be rectified by Apple soon.)

By choosing the **Don't Allow Change** option for **Location Services** in **Content and Privacy Restrictions** (as described in the previous sub-section**),** you will prevent the location tracking from being turned off or cleared by your child.

Rest assured that the location information that is stored on the device is not used by Apple for any advertising and marketing purposes. The location data gathered by the device is encrypted and cannot be read by Apple.

Using iCloud, this **Significant Location** information is sync'd between devices with the same Apple ID.

Protecting your Child's Privacy

Contacts, Calendars, Reminders, Photos, Media & Apple Music

Under **Location Services** in the **Privacy** section of **Content and Privacy Restrictions**, there are other options that allow establishing of privacy restrictions for Contacts, Calendar, Reminders and Photos.

Each of these options in the **Privacy** sections of **Content and Privacy Restrictions** looks very similar to Location Services.

The example shown below right is the **Privacy** settings for the **Contacts** app.

For each of these major apps, once again decide which other apps are allowed to use its data.

In the example shown in the image far right, I have turned off **LinkedIn** and **Messenger** to prevent them accessing **Contacts**.

For each of these areas, tap **Don't Allow Changes** at the top to 'lock in' that area of privacy settings, to prevent any future apps from accessing that data without your permission, and to prevent your child from adjusting these settings from **Settings -> Privacy**.

Bluetooth, Microphone, Speech Recognition

Once again, decide what apps are allowed to use the device's Bluetooth, Microphone and Speech Recognition.

In the example on the right, I have turned off social media app access to my Microphone – figuring you just never know who might be listening!

As with the other areas of settings, tap **Don't Allow Changes** to prevent the child from changing these settings once they have been established and stop future apps from gaining access to these features without your permission.

Protecting your Child's Privacy

Apple Advertising

In **Settings -> Privacy -> Apple** Advertising, there is the option to turn on (or off) something called **Personalised Ads**.

But what does this mean?

As with most businesses, Apple will show you ads in various places – for example, in the App Store, News and Stocks apps.

So that these ads are more relevant to you, there is certain information that Apple collects for this purpose – the detail of which you can see in **View Ad Targeting Information**.

For a child though, you don't necessarily want any such information to be collected – even if it is not shared by Apple with other advertisers or anyone else.

To turn off **Personalised Ads**, go to the **Privacy** section's **Apple Advertising** option in **Content and Privacy Restrictions** and choose **Don't Allow**.

This will turn off the **Personalised Ads** option in **Settings -> Privacy – Apple Advertising** – making it grey/disabled, to prevent your child from turning it back on.

Lock down other aspects of the device

The **'Allow Changes'** section of **Content and Privacy Restrictions** allows a few other areas of the device's setup to be 'locked down'.

For each of the options shown in this section, choose either **Allow Changes** or **Don't Allow** – to specify whether the child can make changes in some key areas.

The idea is to first, <u>on the child's device</u>, sign in to **iCloud** and **iTunes**, set up any mail account/s, decide on whether or not to allow **iMessage**, set up the child's mobile data settings and what Apps can use mobile data (in **Settings->Mobile/Cellular**) and establish the **Background App Refresh** settings (in **Settings-> General**).

Then, come to the **Allow Changes** section – either on the child's device or on the parent's device (if the child is part of your iCloud Family) - to 'lock in' that setup. This will mean that that the child can't change it, set up any new accounts, etc.

Let's look at the key settings in this area.

Passcode Changes

The Passcode Changes option will, if set to **Don't Allow**, hide the **Touch ID & Passcode** (or **Face ID & Passcode**) option from **Settings**, so that changes can't be made to the passcode or the Touch ID/Face ID without parental permission.

This means that you, as a parent, will not be locked out of the child's device due to the child changing the Passcode without permission.

Lock down other aspects of the device

This is one that is worth setting up on the parental devices as well.

By hiding the Passcode area of Settings, a child won't be able to record their own Touch ID / Face ID on that device – something that many children will do if they know the Passcode of that parent-owned device.

It will also avoid the scenario where the child could change the passcode on a device that is not theirs.

Accounts

By choosing **Don't Allow Changes** for **Accounts**, all the settings relating to iCloud, iTunes, mail accounts, iMessage, Facetime and a few other areas will be greyed in **Settings**, preventing any changes.

As with all options in the **Allow Changes** section, if change to an associated setting is required, temporarily change the option back to **Allow Changes** to make the change, then 'lock down' again by changing back to **Don't Allow Changes**.

Lock down other aspects of the device

Mobile Data Use

Don't Allow Changes for **Mobile Data Use** stops the user of the iPhone (or an iPad with a SIM and data allowance) from changing what apps are allowed to use mobile data.

This locks in whatever app settings apply on the device in **Settings -> Mobile**.

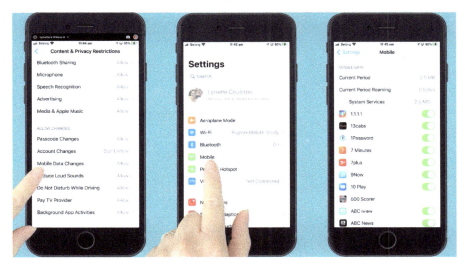

Lock down other aspects of the device

Before choosing **Don't Allow Changes** for **Mobile Data Use**, go to **Settings -> Mobile** (which may be called Cellular or Mobile Data/Cellular Data) and choose what apps can/can't use mobile data on this device.

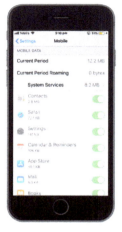

For example, you might want to turn off mobile data for games, social media and streaming/entertainment apps but leave mobile data enabled for things like Maps, Google Maps, and public transport apps.

Once **Don't Allow** is chosen for the **Mobile Data Changes**, the options in **Settings -> Mobile** will be greyed (see image on right), preventing changes by the child.

While we are on the topic of Mobile Data and is usage, another couple of settings are also worth adjusting in **Settings -> Mobile** (Cellular).

They are Wi-Fi Assist, iCloud Drive and iCloud Backup, which you can result in the unintentional use of large amounts of mobile data.

These three settings should be turned off on most devices – unless that device's SIM has a significant mobile data allowance.

58

Lock down other aspects of the device

Reduce Loud Sounds

To protect your child's hearing, it is possible to turn on a Setting to **Reduce Loud Sounds** and then limit the volume when listening using headphones.

This limiting of the volume was previously found in **Settings -> Music**. Since iOS 14, it is now in **Settings -> Sounds & Haptics -> Headphone Safety**.

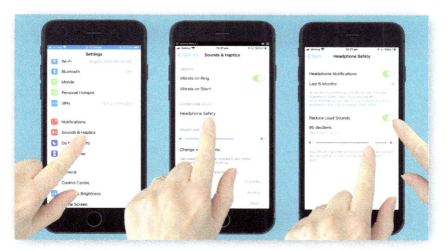

Put some earphones on, put on some music on the device, turn on the **Reduce Loud Sounds** setting and use the slider to set the maximum volume level.

Lock down other aspects of the device

Then, in the **Content and Privacy Restrictions** of **Screen Time**, tap on **Reduce Loud Sound** and choose **Don't Allow** (see previous image).

This will then disable/grey the settings in the **Headphone Safety** option, so that they can't be changed.

Other options in Allow Changes

The remaining options in Allow Changes – **Driving Focus**, **Pay TV Provider** and **Background App Activities** – follow the same principles, in that they allow the parent to lock in the associated settings and prevent changes by the child.

I will skip the **Driving Focus** option (which used to be **Do Not Disturb While Driving**, as shown in in the image below), as this is not relevant to younger children. And the **Pay TV Provider** option is not relevant in Australia.

Background App Refresh is a feature that allows apps to 'refresh their content when on Wi-Fi or mobile data in the background', something that can help apps to load more quickly, but can also use extra battery.

Some apps require this **Background App Refresh** setting to be 'on' for them to work properly. An example of such an app is the Tile app that works with a Tile accessory (for finding your keys).

Lock down other aspects of the device

The settings for **Background App Refresh** can be found in **Settings -> General**.

I recommend turning this feature off for all but essential apps – or turning it off completely.

Then, in the **Content and Privacy Restrictions** of **Screen Time**, tap on **Background App Refresh** and choose **Don't Allow.**

Changing the Screen Time Passcode

If needed, you can the change the Screen Time Passcode very easily.

This is achieved using the **Change Screen Time Passcode** option at the bottom of the main set of **Screen Time** options.

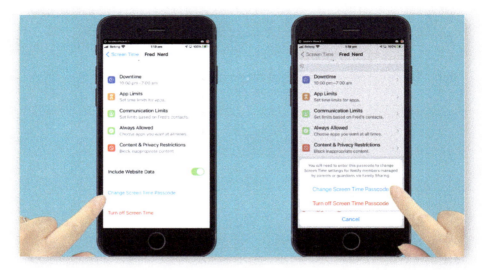

When doing this from the parent's device and changing a child's Screen Time Passcode, you won't need to provide the current Passcode that applies for that child (so make sure your child can't access your device!).

If you choose this option from the child's device – or for Screen Time you have set up for your own device – you will have to provide the current Screen Time Passcode to be able to change this Passcode.

If you don't know this passcode, you can only hope that you have set up the Recovery option (as described earlier) to reset using your Apple ID.

Confine them to a single app – Guided Access

Did you know you can limit your child to using a single App?

I used this feature every day when my son was young. When he wanted to take his iPad to his room at night to 'read', I would 'lock him into' the iBooks (now Books) app.

He then couldn't access any other games (etc.) until I entered a password to remove this lock.

This feature is called **Guided Access** and is available from **Settings -> Accessibility**.

Guided Access is under the **General** section of Accessibility, near the bottom. (Note that, in iOS 13 and earlier, Accessibility settings were found under the General option).

Turn **Guided Access** to 'On' (green), then set a Passcode in **Passcode Settings** – one that your children won't know or be able to guess.

Choose whether Face ID / Touch ID can also be used in addition to the Passcode – which you would only do when setting up Guided Access on your own device.

Hot Tip: I recommend that you use the same Passcode here as used for *Screen Time* – otherwise you may find yourself unable to remember this additional password. Given that this Guided Access passcode is a 6-digit passcode, perhaps just add two zeros to the end.

'Confine them to a single app – Guided Access

This will be enough to get you started. When you are ready to 'lock your child in' to a particular App, open that App.

<u>Once in the app</u>, turn on **Guided Access** in one of the following ways

- Triple-click the Home Button if the device has one OR
- Triple-click the on-off button (i.e. sleep/wake switch) if there is no Home Button

Note that **Guided Access** will only be able to be activated when an App is open, not when the Home Screen is in view.

Some options will then appear at the top and bottom. Just tap **Start** at the top right to enter **Guided Access** mode.

Your child won't be able to exit the app.

The only way to exit will be for you to triple-press the **Home Button / On-Off Button**, then enter your **Guided Access** passcode (or use Face ID / Touch ID, if this has been enabled).

'Confine them to a single app – Guided Access

When this is done, an **End** option will appear at the top left to exit **Guided Access** mode. **Resume** will appear at top right, to allow the app to re-enter **Guided Access** mode.

Customise Guided Access

There are some additional features worth considering before you start a **Guided Access** session for an App.

Tap **Options** at bottom left to view the set of options available.

These options allow you to control things like whether buttons are functional during Guided Access and whether screen touch/tap is available.

Most importantly, also here is the ability to set a time limit.

'Confine them to a single app – Guided Access

Set a Time Limit

The **Time Limit** option is an extremely handy feature that allows the setting of a time limit for the child's use of the app.

For example, setting a time limit of 3 minutes will mean that, at the 3-minute mark, the child will no longer be able to continue using the app.

When time is up, a screen like that on the right will appear and no other activity will be possible until the **Guided Access** Passcode (or, if enabled, Touch ID/Face ID) is entered after triple-clicking the Home/On-Off button.

'Rope Off' certain areas of the screen

Before 'starting' a **Guided Access** session for a child, you can 'circle' certain areas of the screen that you don't want your child to access – options that you don't want then to tap.

This will then put a shaded area over those parts of the screen.

When **Guided Access** is started, if your child taps that area of the screen, nothing will happen.

For example, if the child is reading a book in **Guided Access** mode (in Books), circle all areas that would allow the child to exit the book you want them to be reading.

'Confine them to a single app – Guided Access

If you forget your Guided Access Passcode

Don't stress – a 'forced re-boot' will get the device out of Guided Access mode.

(If you are not sure how to do this, refer to the iTandCoffee guide **Introduction to the iPad – A Guided Tour**, which covers all sorts of basics like this.)

A warning if your child is older or more 'savvy'

If your child knows how to do a 'forced re-boot' of the device, this will get them out of the **Guided Access** mode and allow them to get back to the lock screen, then **Home Screen**.

But you will know that they have done this.

The App will no longer be in **Guided Access** mode, indicating that they have '*forced*' the device to exit this mode.

Does your family have a case of iCloud Confusion?

First, what is an Apple ID?

An Apple ID is the email address used to register an Account with Apple, where this account may be used for the **Media and Purchases**, for **iCloud**, for **iMessage**, and for **Facetime** – for some or all these features.

Historically, the Apple ID used for the **iTunes and App Store** has often been shared by more than one family member, so that purchases of Music, Movies, Apps and Books can also be shared. This is certainly what we have done in this household for many years.

iCloud/iMessage/Facetime Apple ID should belong to one person only

The **Apple ID** used for **iCloud** (and for iMessage and Facetime) is not one that should be shared with other members of the household.

The **iCloud Apple ID** is used to synchronise data between that individual's devices (e.g. Contacts, Calendar Entries, Reminders, Notes, Passwords), to **Back Up** the individual's devices, to sync and/or stream photos between devices, and much more.

Shared Apple IDs used for iCloud, Facetime and Messages can result in mixed up data, lost data, lack of space in iCloud for backups, mixed up photos, shared call history, family members receiving each other's texts and Facetime calls, and more.

Many families find that they are not set up correctly since, historically, it used to be impossible to set up an Apple ID for a child.

In the past, setting up an iCloud account or iTunes and App Store account required that the child's age was 13 or over, so it was necessary to tell a 'white lie' about the child's age in order to set up an account.

In so many families, parents simply used their own Apple ID on their child's device.

In recent years however, Apple has introduced a solution to this problem - allowing 'child' Apple Accounts to be created by parents, for children under 13. We'll cover this shortly.

Does your family have a case of iCloud Confusion?

"Hey, you, get offa my cloud!"

If multiple people share a same Apple ID, one needs to 'own' that Apple ID, and others need to sign out of that Apple ID on all their devices. This is done from **Settings -> [your-name]**, by choosing **Sign Out** at the bottom of that screen.

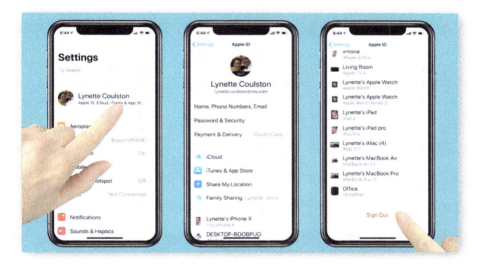

If the device was previously signed in to **Find My**, you will need to first sign out using the password applicable to the Apple ID.

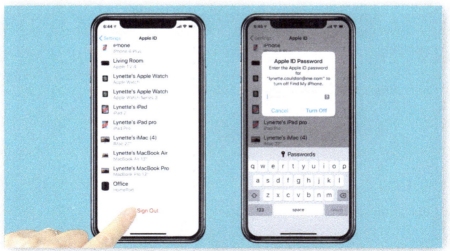

Does your family have a case of iCloud Confusion?

You will then be asked to choose any of the data from that iCloud account that you wish to keep on the device (which you will subsequently merge into the new/separate iCloud account).

Generally, for a child, you will probably choose to leave all of these settings turned off – unless there is something that they need to keep a copy of.

You may also be asked what to do about low resolution versions of photos that are not stored on this device – that are instead stored in iCloud.

We won't go into the topic of iCloud Photos in this guide, as it gets quite complex. Refer to iTandCoffee's separate user guide (The Comprehensive Guide to iCloud) for more information about this topic. Or contact iTandCoffee for assistance.

Once the **Keep a Copy Of** options have been selected, choose **Sign Out** at top right to detatch this device from that incorrect Apple ID.

Your iCloud Family

In iOS 8 in 2014, Apple introduced the concept of an iCloud Family.

This was initially focused on sharing purchases between members of the one family and allowing parents to set up Apple accounts for their children.

iCloud Family has since extended to allowing sharing of iCloud storage, subscription services like Apple TV and Apple Music, Location Sharing, parental control of child devices, and more.

Becoming an iCloud Family

One person in the family sets themselves up as the 'organiser' of the family, and then invites other members of the family to join the iCloud Family, assuming the other family members already have their own Apple ID.

Setting up your iCloud Family is done from **Settings -> *your-name* -> Family Sharing**

Once you have turned on this feature, you can then invite others to join your Family.

This can be done by sending them an email, a text, or Airdropping the request to them (see image on next page). They can then use the link provided to join your family from their own device, by signing in with their Apple ID details.

Your iCloud Family

If they are present with you, you can choose the **Invite in Person** option and get them to sign in with their Apple account details.

A child who is 13 or over can create their own Apple ID as part of the 'sign-in' process on their device, from the option at the very top of the Settings app.

If the child is younger than 13, a parent can create the account for the child.

Creating an Apple ID for a child

In cases where the family member is a child and does not yet have their own Apple ID, there is the option from the **Invite People to your Family** screen for the organiser to choose to **Create an Account for a Child**.

You can also come back later and add your child's account from the **Add a Family Member** option that is available once your Family has been created, from **Settings -> *your-name* -> Family Sharing** (see next image)

Your iCloud Family

The **Create Apple ID for a child** screen will appear.

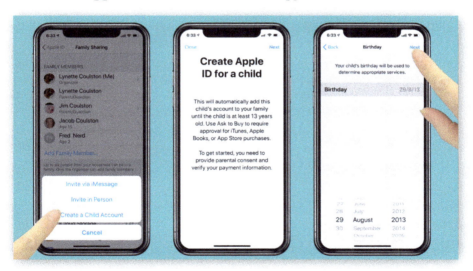

- Choose **Next** to proceed.
- First, enter the child's birthday
- Verify the CCV for your Family credit card
- Enter the child's first and last name

Your iCloud Family

- Choose an email address for the child – it will end in @icloud.com. The name before the @ will have to be one that no-one else has registered.

- Then choose a password (enter it twice). It will need to have at least one capital and one number and have at least 8 characters.
- Next comes the secret question and answer setup. The questions can be hard to answer from your child's point of view – so you may need to give your own answers. Make sure you note whether you use upper or lower case in the answers. It is a good idea to store the answers in your Password Safe.
- You will need to agree to Apple's terms and conditions more than once.
- Just keep following the instructions and choosing the option at top right to step though all the required steps.

At the end of all those steps, you will have an Apple account (Apple ID) created for your child that can then be used on their Apple devices for various things that you choose to either allow or disallow.

This Apple ID does give them an email address that can be used on their device, but you can choose whether or not you enable the Mail feature of the account from the iCloud settings on the child's device.

Your iCloud Family

Ask To Buy

You will see that the final step of creating the child's account will be to set the **Ask to Buy** option to provide you, as parent, with control over your child's downloads and purchases.

After you have completed setup of the child's Apple ID, you can then adjust the **Ask to Buy** settings from **Settings -> *your-name* -> Family Sharing**, in the **Shared with your Family** section that is below the list of family member names.

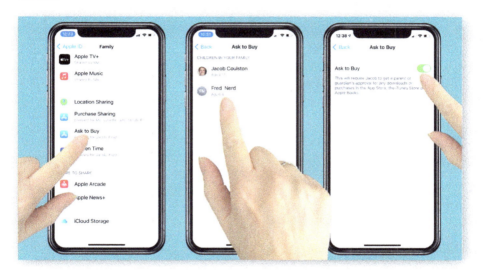

The **Ask to Buy** option provides the list of under 18 family member names. Tap each to set or remove the **Ask to Buy** for that child.

Then, when the child attempts to download a free app or purchase an app, you will get a notification on your own Apple device, asking you to approve this acquisition.

Purchases will be made using the credit card linked to the Family (unless that child has some iTunes credit on their own account).

You will need to enter your Apple ID's password to approve the app download/purchase.

Your iCloud Family

Now set up that Apple ID on the Child's device

You will then need to go to the child's device and sign in using this new Apple ID (to set up iCloud on that device).

This is done from the first option in the **Settings** app (which should give you the option to sign in).

Setting up and understanding iCloud is the topic of another iTandCoffee Guide, so will not be covered further here.

Contact iTandCoffee to get a copy of **The Comprehensive Guide to iCloud** guide or to request further assistance with this.

Now you can set up your child's Screen Time from your own device

Once your child has been added as a member of your Family, you will then be able to manage that child's Screen Time from your own device/s. Their name will appear in **Settings -> Screen Time**, as shown earlier on page 17 – allowing you to control most of the parental controls for **all** their devices remotely.

What do you want to share with your family?

The **Shared with your Family** section of the Family Sharing settings allows you to choose what you wish to share with your family.

Certain Apple service subscriptions that you have can be shared with the other family members, as can purchases of Apps, Books, Music, Movies, etc (**Purchase Sharing**).

The **More to Share** section at the very bottom allows you to share your iCloud Storage as well if you subscribe to the 200GB option or higher – so that you don't have to pay for separate storage for each family member.

(Note. When you share iCloud storage, you still have separate areas for each person's storage. No-one else from the family will have access to your own iCloud data.)

Your iCloud Family

In iOS/iPadOS 16, there is now a **Family Checklist** option – providing a list of things to consider and review

Those little hackers will find a way

As kids get a bit older, they will inevitably look for ways to get around restrictions that prevent them from doing what they want to do! This can become a real challenge for parents who are often not as tech-savvy as their kids. Here are some ways your child can get around the controls that you set up.

Getting around the 'Ask to buy' restriction

One of the benefits of the iCloud Family feature is the ability to share any content purchased by any family member.

However, this can also be a disadvantage when it comes to children sharing the Family account.

Once an app has been purchased by ANY family member, it is then available to be downloaded by the child as well – without any authorization being required by the parent (as long as it is not restricted by the 'age restrictions' set up in **Content and Privacy Restrictions**).

This means that Facebook, Instagram, Snapchat, and many other apps may be available for your child to download and use without your knowledge.

To solve this problem, you need to 'hide' any apps that have been 'purchased' by the other Family members, but that you do not want the younger children to download.

This is achieved by visiting the **App Store** app on the parent's iPad or iPhone (or on the device belonging to the family member who purchased the app) and going to the 'Purchased' view.

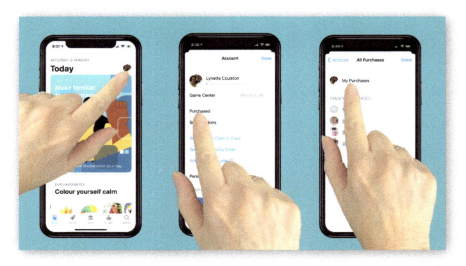

78

Those little hackers will find a way

The **Purchased** option can be found in the account area of the App Store, accessed by tapping the 'profile' circle at top right, then the **Purchased** option (see previous image).

You can then tap on any of the people listed to see the purchases/downloads by each person. (From here, you can choose to download any of their purchased apps for no cost.)

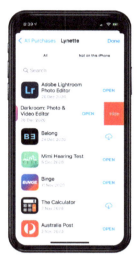

Your own purchases/downloads can be viewed from the **My Purchases** option in **Purchased.**

To 'Hide' an app that you do not wish other family members to see or be able to download, simply swipe from right-to-left on an App, and tap **Hide**.

The app will magically disappear from your list of **Purchased** apps, and no-one else will be able to see it and download it from this area.

Can you 'unhide' hidden apps?

A Hidden app can now be 'unhidden'.

This has not been possible for many years, but iOS/iPadOS 15 delivered a fix for this previously long term 'broken' feature.

'Unhide' an app by visiting **Settings-> *your-name*-> Media and Purchases ->View Account ->Hidden Purchases** and choosing **Unhide**.

Those little hackers will find a way

Getting around App Limits

Pretty early in the life of Screen Time, kids found that they could get around the time limits set by parents for particular apps by deleting the app and then re-installing it (which doesn't require **Ask to buy** permission).

Assuming that app uses iCloud Drive, the child will not lose the history of data stored by that app – but the re-installation resets the clock as far as the time limit goes.

To prevent this, you can block deleting of Apps in the **iTunes & App Store** option of **Content and Privacy Restrictions**, as described earlier on page 36.

Time Travel to avoid App Limits and Downtime

To get around Downtime, kids have been known to change the time zone of the device from **Settings -> General -> Date & Time**.

This can be prevented by ensuring that you choose **Don't Allow Changes** for **Location Services** in the Privacy section of **Content and Privacy Restrictions** (refer page 47).

Accessing YouTube when it is blocked

If a child is desperate to watch YouTube, they can bypass your controls and still watch a YouTube video if they receive a link to that video via iMessage.

It is essential to set up parental controls for YouTube itself, so that your child doesn't access inappropriate content there. We won't cover this in this guide though, as this gets into a whole other territory.

If you are not sure you can trust your child on iMessage, you can always make the choice to disable it by not allowing your child to sign in to iMessage with their Apple ID, then choosing **Don't Allow** for **Accounts**, as described on page 56.

Factory Reset

A really tech-savvy child can perform a **Factory Reset** of the device, which will clear all the Screen Time controls that have been set.

One way around this is to never give your child the password for their Apple ID – which must be entered to turn off the activation lock associated with **Find My**.

Those little hackers will find a way

Then, even if they do a factory reset, they will be blocked from setting up the device again because they don't know that password to get past the activation lock that still exists if a device is reset.

Your Child has access to your own device

If you child knows your device passcode or has unsupervised access to your iPhone, iPad, or Mac, they could turn off their own Screen Time from your device, remove the Screen Time passcode, or even change it so that you no longer know the correct passcode.

Hacking a Screen Time Passcode

There is also software that can be purchased for a computer that allows for 'hacking' of the Screen Time passcode – something that can be necessary for parents who have lost that passcode!

If a child has access to a computer and the ability to purchase such software, they can do a backup of the iPhone or iPad to the computer, then use the purchased software to discover the Screen Time passcode.

Changing their Screen Time settings from your device

If you child knows the password for your own device and if you have allowed the use of Touch ID for adjusting the Screen Time settings or have not set a Screen Time passcode for your own device, your child may be able to change the Screen Time passcode for their own devices or turn off the passcode – or turn off their Screen Time.

With your device passcode, they can even change your Apple account password from your device – which could give them the ability to change the Screen Time Passcode that you have set for your own device (and then theirs).

I know this sounds extreme, but iTandCoffee has seen it all in families.

Some children are so addicted to their technology that they will do ANYTHING to gain the access they desire.

Those little hackers will find a way

By-passing limits on Texting/Messaging

If a child visits their Contacts app and chooses the Share option from there to Share a Contact Card, they get the ability to send a message to anyone. They can delete the Contact Card in the message and enter anything as the message.

Unfortunately, this seems a real oversight by Apple, one that there appears to be no way of blocking.

And I'm sure there are others ...

Over time, savvy kids will find other 'hacks. If a child is determined to get around restrictions that are set, then they will.

It's worth Googling something like 'screen time hacks' to find out the latest ways that kids are by-passing controls.

Of course, nothing can replace parental oversight, open and honest communication, and teaching your child to self-regulate – especially as children get older.

Make Sure 'Find My' is Enabled

Apple provides a great feature of iCloud that allows you to find a device that is perhaps lost, or to locate the person associated with that device.

It is called **Find My**, and is supported by the **Find My** app.

Enabling Find My

For this feature to work, you must enable an iCloud setting on the child's device, called **Find My** - which is found in **Settings -> *your-name* -> Find My**

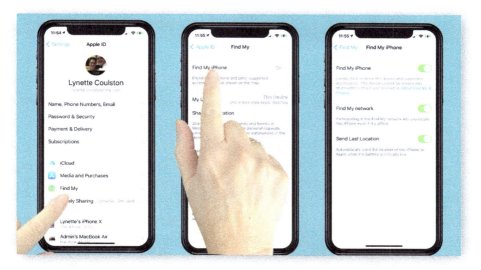

Turn on all the options in the **Find My** option, so that you have the best chance of finding a lost device.

If a device is lost, go to the **Find My** app, and tap the Devices option along the bottom (see image on next page).

This will show the list of devices that are associated with your Family - for those people who have agreed to share their location with you (which, if you have set this up, will include your children's devices).

(Note. A new option now appears at the bottom of the screen in Find My – the **Items** option, an option not showing in the screen images below. We will not cover this feature in this guide, but it relates to Air Tags associated user's Apple account.)

Make Sure 'Find My' is Enabled

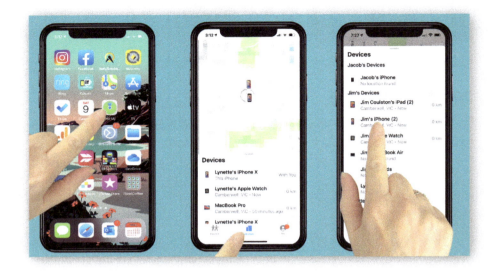

Tap on the device that is lost.

Hopefully that device will show on a map. If it is nearby, choose the **Play Sound** option to try to locate the device. A sound will be played even if the device is in 'mute' mode.

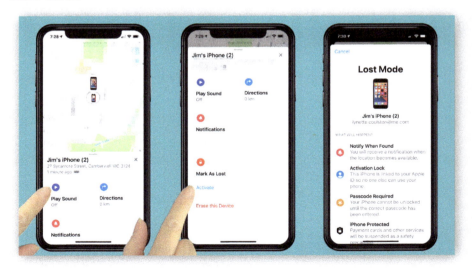

Make Sure 'Find My' is Enabled

If the device has been left somewhere or is just lost, choose to **Mark as Lost** by choosing the **Activate** option under that heading. The screen that appears tells you what will happen when you turn on this feature – how the device will be

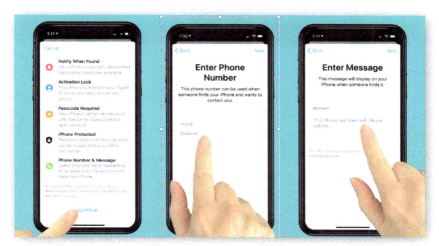

protected and how a notification can be received when the device's location becomes available.

Choose **Continue**, then enter a contact phone number that the finder can ring. (Hint: Don't use the device's phone number!) Then choose **Next** and enter a message for the finder.

A summary of the provided information is shown, with the option to **Activate** the **Lost Mode**.

When the device is retrieved, simply enter the device's passcode to turn off the **Lost Mode**.

If the device is stolen, the fact that **Find My** has been enabled for the device will prevent that person from ever being able to use the device if they don't know your iCloud account password.

If your device has truly been stolen and/or is not retrievable, choose the **Erase this Device** option (which is found under the option for Lost Mode).

If the lost device is not one that you can see via the **Find My** app, sign in to person's Apple ID via **iCloud.com**.

Even if you don't have the device to enable you to obtain

Make Sure 'Find My' is Enabled

the two-factor authentication code, there is the **Find iPhone** option at the bottom that of the two-factor authentication window that appears after you enter your password – allowing allows you to access the **Find Devices** features via the web browser, to locate any device associated with your Apple ID.

You will be taken to a sign-in screen for the Find Devices feature of iCloud.

Enter your password, to see a map that shows the location of the devices.

Choose device by click **All Devices** at the top to select the applicable device.

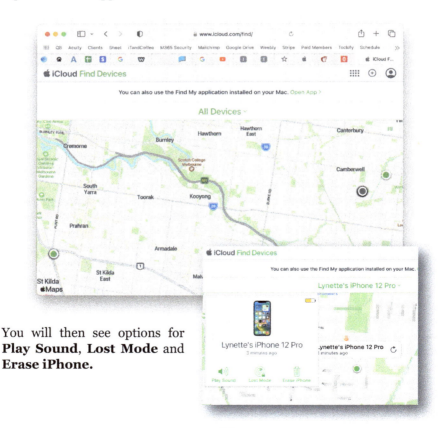

You will then see options for **Play Sound**, **Lost Mode** and **Erase iPhone.**

Can your child see all your Passwords?

If you use iCloud, you have the option to allow iCloud to store passwords to various online accounts, Wi-Fi networks and more.

This is by enabling an iCloud feature called **Keychain** in **Settings —> *your-name* -> iCloud**

This setting means that you may have a heap of password stored in your **Settings** app, accessible by entering your device passcode or using Touch ID / Face ID.

Go to **Settings -> Passwords** to see the list of stored passwords. Tap on any of these and enter your device passcode (or Touch ID / Face ID) to view the password for any of the items listed.

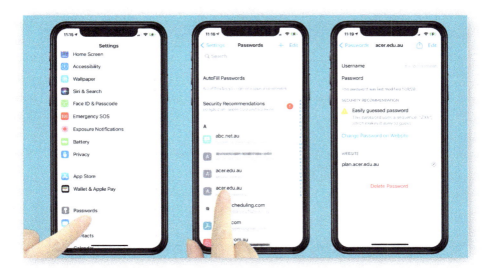

If your child knows your passcode or has stored their fingerprint on that device, they will also have access to ALL these saved passwords.

This is yet another good reason to ensure that your device passcode is not disclosed to your child – and for hiding the Passcode settings, as described on page 55.

Let's talk about iMessage and Facetime

Understanding iMessage

iMessage provides a similar capability to that provided by a mobile phone's SMS capability.

iMessage is a feature of the Messages app. The Messages app is clever enough to handle both SMS and iMessage messages in one place.

Green speech bubbles represent SMS's; blue represent iMessages.

The key difference between an SMS and an iMessage is that iMessage uses the internet to send the message and does not require a phone with a SIM card and SMS allowance.

It is the same sort of thing as Facebook/Instagram Messenger, Whatsapp, and various other messaging apps. All you need to send an iMessage is internet access via Wi-Fi or mobile data.

Then, it is possible to share text, photos, videos, audio, and your location with other iMessage users.

How to turn on iMessage in the Messages app

For iMessage to work, iMessage must be turned on in **Settings -> Messages.**

For devices that don't have a SIM card to be able to use iMessage, the device must be signed in to iMessage with the user's Apple ID (again, from **Settings -> Messages**).

Make sure you set up iMessage correctly

Make sure that you do not use a shared Apple ID for iMessage.

It is extremely common for family members to set up iMessage incorrectly and end up getting each other's messages – sometimes causing all manner of upheaval in a family.

Let's talk about iMessage and Facetime

iMessage supports 'group' conversations.

By addressing an iMessage to several people who all have iMessage enabled, everyone sees everyone else's responses.

While this is a great feature most of the time, it is easy to get into hot water with this feature. It is very easy to respond to whole group when you think you are responding to an individual.

Both adults and children need to consider the words they use in an iMessage.

Once the Send option is chosen, there is no way of 'recalling' what has been sent.

Should you restrict iMessage on a child's device?

This all depends on your reasons for giving your child an i-Device in the first place.

If the main intent is to listen to music and play games, or if your child is very young, you may want to consider restricting iMessage.

Consider blocking iMessage during **Downtime** – and using the **Communication Limits** to ensure that they can only have contact with people you approve. And you can set an **App Limit** on the Messages app.

If you don't want your kids using iMessage, be aware that there are many other messaging and chatting apps in Apps store – so you will need to ensure that these apps are not being used in place of iMessage.

Some parents find it handy for kids to have iMessage, as a way of keeping in touch when the child is not with them.

And then there's Facetime

Would you allow a boy in your 12-year-old daughter's bedroom at night, alone with the door closed?

If your child has an iPad or iPhone, they may be able to do this without your knowledge – maybe not physically, but via video link.

Let's talk about iMessage and Facetime

Many parents ban computers from bedrooms, but don't consider Apple mobile devices to be the same danger as the computer.

With Wi-Fi access, the iPhone and iPad are really just small, powerful computers, with many of the same features as a computer – and more!

Video chatting brings truly brings new challenges when it comes to privacy considerations, letting people into your home in a very real way, and sometimes when you don't realize that they are there.

I have walked into my own daughter's bedroom in my PJ's, only to be met by a boyfriend on the computer screen – who has seen me in my 'full glory'. Great!

It is important to consider rules around use of Facetime by children, and even consider restricting access to this feature for younger children.

How to turn on/off Facetime

For Facetime to work, Facetime must be enabled from **Settings -> Facetime**.

Simply turn off the setting there to disable it, then choose **Don't Allow** for **Accounts** in **Content and Privacy Restrictions** (as described on page 56).

Use other Screen Time features to limit Facetime use

If you don't want your child using Facetime without your permission, turn it off in the **Content and Privacy Restrictions** of **Screen Time** (see page 37) or, as for Messages, consider blocking Facetime during **Downtime** – and using the **Communication Limits** to ensure that they can only have contact with people you approve.

And, of course, you can also set an **App Limit** for the Facetime app.

A very quick look at Restricting YouTube

I won't go into any great detail in this guide about YouTube, as our focus is on the built-in features and apps on the iPad and iPhone.

YouTube Kids for Younger Children

For younger children, consider only allowing the **YouTube Kids** app, which is specifically designed for children up to the age of 12 (as YouTube is supposed to only be suitable for children over 13).

Just be very aware that YouTube and Google are very focused on collecting data about your child for advertising and targeting purposes. (YouTube Kids will not collect such data due to privacy regulations relating to children.)

Restricted Mode

Up until recently, all that was available to parents of YouTube users was something called **Restricted Mode**, which prevented your child from seeing 'adult' content.

See the images below for the steps involved in setting up **Restricted Mode** in the YouTube App.

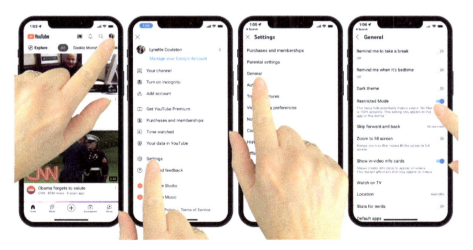

Here's where to find more information about this feature.

https://support.google.com/youtube/answer/174084

A very quick look at Restricting YouTube

New Supervised Accounts for YouTube

In early 2021, Google introduced some new controls for YouTube – called Supervised Accounts.

In a similar way to Apple's Family setup, Google allows you to set up parent and child Google accounts, where the child account is managed by the parent.

This setup is from **https://myaccount.google.com/people-and-sharing**, or from the **Family Link** app. We will just look at the web browser screens in this guide, but similar options can be found in Family Link.

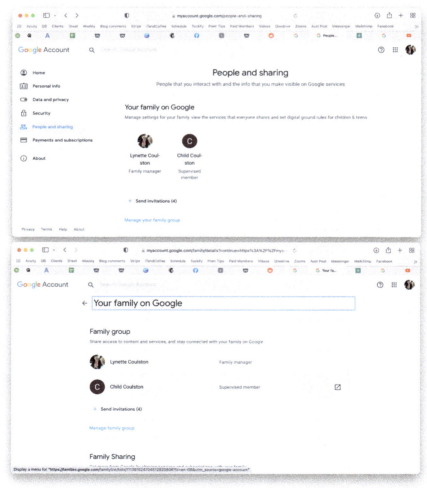

A very quick look at Restricting YouTube

Choose **Manage your family group** then select the child account to be configured. This gives a screen that has **Parental settings**, one of which is **Settings on YouTube**

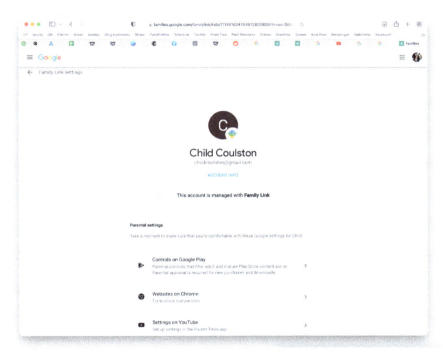

The **Settings on YouTube** option gives the screen on the right.

Selecting the second option (right) gives the below disclaimer. Choose **Select**.

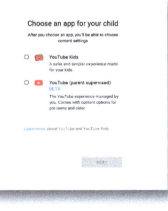

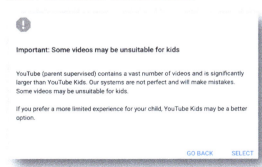

A very quick look at Restricting YouTube

Then choose the level of control according to the age of your child.

Each option describes the sort of content that will be available under that setting.

The third option has the following description. Choose **Select** to confirm.

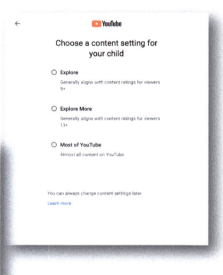

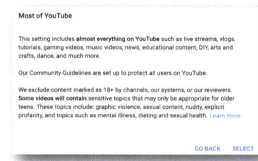

The child's YouTube app will need to be signed in as their own 'child' account, in order that the settings you have establish are applied to that app.

If you need any further help with settings relating to YouTube, Google or Android devices – especially how to set up your family on Google - iTandCoffee can assist through a remote or in-person support appointment.

Visit www.itandcoffee.com.au/appointment-request for more information.

Yes, it's hard to keep up!

If you feel like things move too fast for you to keep up, **YOU ARE NOT ALONE**!

When my eldest child was young, Facebook was the key app for kids and was the main concern among parents.

This changed so much over the young lives of my 4 children, the youngest of which is now a late teen.

Instagram and Snapchat became way more popular with children. And Tik Tok has become a phenomenon with not just children.

A huge variety have come and gone as popular apps over this time: My Space, Kik Messenger, Ask.fm, Sararah, Musical.ly (now Tik Tok), Yubo (was Yellow – Tinder for Kids!).

I still check in regularly with my own children, friends and relatives about the apps that younger kids use most to communicate with friends, and what games are most popular.

And it changes every time I ask! That game that is so popular today is 'old hat' tomorrow.

When my own kids were younger, I would always get them to take me through the app/game and talk about any potential dangers they can see. I would even try out what apps I could (although most games were beyond me!).

I do know it is a constant battle.

It's such a tough era to be a parent, with the complications of technology and its impact on our kids. I am glad mine are now past that stage.

All I can say to those of you with younger children is GOOD LUCK!

If you would like to see a range of articles that cover all sorts of topics about kids on technology – dangerous apps, social media apps, messaging apps, other third party parental control services, parental controls on Microsoft, Google and Mac, how to set household-wide parental controls and more, visit

www.itandcoffee.com.au/cybersafety

And, of course, if you need help with managing your family's technology (either remotely or in person), contact iTandCoffee at enquiry@itandcoffee.com.au or visit www.itandcoffee.com.au/appointment-request to book an appointment.

www.ingramcontent.com/pod-product-compliance
Lightning Source LLC
LaVergne TN
LVHW011802070326
832902LV00025B/4610